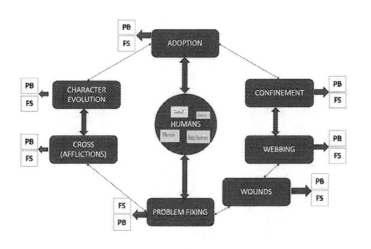

JOSEPH'S DIARY

(MY JOURNEY IN PROGRESS)

AZUBUIKE ONYEKWULUJE JOSEPH

WESTBOW
PRESS®
A DIVISION OF THOMAS NELSON
& ZONDERVAN

WestBow Press books may be ordered through booksellers or by contacting:

WestBow Press
A Division of Thomas Nelson & Zondervan
1663 Liberty Drive
Bloomington, IN 47403
www.westbowpress.com
844-714-3454

ISBN: 978-1-6642-8426-5 (sc)
ISBN: 978-1-6642-8425-8 (e)

Print information available on the last page.

WestBow Press rev. date: 02/24/2023

"EVERYBODY HAS A STORY, AND THE STORY IS YOUR LIFE STORY. IT'S A LIFE STORY DEVOTIONAL AND YOU NEED TO LET PEOPLE KNOW HOW YOU'RE CHANGED."

Margo Fieseler, author of *Unwavering*

The author wishes to dedicate this piece to my parent who relentlessly worked hard to train me into the person I am today. And to my great friends

CONTENTS

ACKNOWLEDGMENT

The author would like to express his gratitude to the following persons:

Tracy Pirie
Snr Prophet T.B Joshua (Mentor)
Mrs. Evelyn Joshua (Mother of faith)
Dr. Martin Anagboso (Mentor)
Tochukwu Onyekwuluje (Uncle)
Mr Asika Onyekwuluje (Dad)
Mrs. Cecilia Onyekwuluje (Mother)
Chukwuebuka Onyekwuluje (Brother)
Ogechukwu Onyekwuluje (Sister)
Dr. Godwin Chimara (Mentor)

because of their support in prayer and counseling.

LETTER TO MY READERS

Hi, my readers. I want to use this opportunity to thank you for getting hold of this book. It is with pleasure, and I hope this book meets your expectations. Relax and enjoy reading and take inspiration from me. Everything might not resonate with you, but I promise you will learn vital lessons from my mistakes and struggles in my journey. Whatever you are going through as a Christian, or non-Christian, or whatever religion you belong be strong. Someone who is up there is watching everyone and He only knows what you are going through, and He is able and capable of seeing you through. Follow my story, and I promise you will be glad you did. Also, messages I received from my Father (Jesus Christ) were included in this book.

The result I would want my readers to have are success, absolute peace, joy, and above all to discover their true value the way it should be.

I am not writing this story to promote myself either. However, I felt someone out there could be going through the same thing I went through. This story of mine would bring encouragement to the person, not to give up but persevere in hard times, which will come and leave at the right time. Have a good read.

WHAT THE BOOK IS ABOUT - THEMES OF MY MESSAGE

This book culminates my story and journey in life. A man purified through suffering who tries to search for meaning and purpose in life. Also, desire to become who I was meant to be as a person and who God created me to be. Seeing myself the way God sees me and not what others feel I would become. The book is not meant to promote me but to share my life experiences with someone who might be going through the same thing I went through. My past, present, and future were enumerated but not in their entirety. Joseph Diary is specifically meant for a person who felt his/her life would move in a certain way but ended up in a different direction because of vicissitudes of life which he/she of course cannot control. My bigger idea is how my life was shaped due to my experience and I desire other people's life to also change because of this story. Enjoy your reading.

WHY THIS BOOK - VALUE

The reason for this book is to bring hope to someone who is about to give up his or her dreams or goals in life. Life circumstances or challenges sometimes tend to impede our forward movement but the ability to see them as an opportunity to a greater height would give one an upward motion. Pick up again and run with your goals. If you have not experienced any challenge or obstacle, remember that no one is exempted from all these. Hope and complete trust in God (Jesus the savior of mankind) can enable us to go through all these challenges and come out victoriously. Take encouragement from God's word from James 1: 2-3, which says, Dear brothers and sisters, when troubles of any kind come your way, consider it an opportunity for great joy, 3. For you know that when your faith is tested, your endurance has a chance to grow. This book is for someone who has fashioned their life in a certain way but ended up differently, may be because of the unfairness or vicissitudes of life that happened unexpectedly.

PAST (PERSONAL ORIGIN STORY)

As a child, growing up in the city of Enugu was fun and exuberating. Enugu happens to be one of the southeast states situated in Nigeria as I can remember; life was so beautiful as a child. I had everything going well.

Lest I forget, Before I move on with the trailblazer, let me tell you about my village. I am a native of Umunya in the Oyi Local Government (LGA) area of Anambra state.

Umunya is an Olu Town and one of the five settlements that make up the Oyi Local Government Area (LGA) in the Nigerian state of Anambra. Ifite-Dunu, Awkuzu, Nteje, Nkwelle-Ezunaka, Ogbunike, and Umudioka are its six neighbors. Umudioka and Ifite-Dunu, are both located in the Dunukofia LGA, which is in the south. Nteje and Nkwelle-Ezunaka in the northern region. Ogbunike is in the west while Awkuzu is in the east. Streams naturally mark the borders, except for the Nkwelle-Ezunaka border, where a large area of Umunya heath, including Oli-Omoto, Ogwugwu-Obo, Ugwueze, etc., bridged the Kpokili River. Almost all ten of Umunya's communities has their freshwater springs. The town's economy is predominantly agriculture because it is blessed with fertile soil.

The 10 villages that make up the town are Ezi-Umunya,

Okpu, Ojobi, Umuebo, Amaezike, Ajakpani, Odumodu-Ani, Isioye, and Odumodu-Enu. All Gadite H/Igbos have a tri-partite ancestry known in anthropological history as ERI-AKA Igbo, which is subdivided into the settlements of Ezi, Ifite, and Ikenga.

I wouldn't go further without telling you about the myths and the related history of my town. It goes thus, the father of ERI, the ancestor of the Igbos of Guinea Forest West Africa, and the creator of Umunya is known as Nya. According to the legend, Isi-Ogwugwu, a swift river, joined River Omambala and at that point, it covered the present-day Umunya region. It was thought that Isi-Ogwugwu was responsible for the region's current rolling topography. Storytellers frequently attribute this narrative to the picturesque depression of Urunda toward Ogbunike.

A moving flash in the river that followed an uncommon wave swirl hit Nya on a particular Eke day while he was ferrying farmers and fishermen through the magnificent Isi-Ogwugwu water route, according to the legend. Nya stopped working in awe of a river goddess, whom he thought was traveling to the western Eke market, due to the extraordinary character of the "twist and twirl" of the flash. He had a vision of a stone that would serve as the foundation for a farming village that would eventually become his people as he stepped outside to rest.

Additionally, when he opened his eyes, he saw that the river had drained further than where he had tethered his canoe. He interpreted this as a validation of his dream. Consequently, he made this location, "Ilo-Umuebo," his home. The Ilo-Umuebo is currently Umunya's High Justice's main court, where the truth must be told. He built the neighborhood that is now known as Umunya (UMU NYA/NNYA, or "Children of Nya") by bringing his family and friends.

Umunya was destroyed by invaders from the Igbo interior before the arrival of the white man, most likely in the 13th or 14th century. The first attack, which was viewed as an internal conspiracy, destroyed the Ezi sub-precursor group's villages,

2

Adagbe-Mpo, Mponenem, Oviabuzo, Ezi-Oli, and Okpuru. Until equivalent sacrifices were performed through the installation of the Ana god and Ana Priest, Nwakonobi, to replace those killed in the mayhem, this incident was viewed with animosity.

At the beginning of the 16th century, Igboegbuna Odezulu-Igbo Onenulu I founded the Hebraic Ozo Tradition, exposing Umunya to **the Nri**-established leadership style. He buried a mystery piece of "Lapis Lazuli" beneath the Obi at Umuebo that Nya had originally guarded and brought with him. He was the first chieftain of the warrior Dynasty that ruled Umunya until the colonial authority established warrants in the 20th century.

Like how the Jewish cabala is practiced, the Ozo is a trend in people's lives. It turns becomes the center for Umunya tradition and culture. When men were "bold and prepared" and ready to hold the majestic truths, they were the only ones who could use the term "Nze" (one who avoids evil).

Similar to its neighboring towns, Umunya is divided into the three socio-political groups known as Ezi, Ifite, and Ikenga. It is claimed that the Eri-Igbo are distinguished by this organizational structure. The elders of Umunya decided on restructuring in response to Ezi-imminent Umunya's extinction, combining the remaining Ezi-Umunya with the former Ifite villages of Okpu, Amaezike, and Ukunu to form a new village grouping known as Akanano. What was left of Ifite—Ojobi, Umuebo, Ajakpani, and Isioye—became known going forward as Okpoko, while Odumodu-Ani and Odumodu-Enu continued to be known as Ikenga. Akanano, Okpoko, and Ikenga are the three units that makeup Umunya, and they serve both administrative and defense roles.

Now back to my story, let me not bore you with too much history of mine. Let's continue the story, my dad, at the time, worked in First Bank in Nigeria (FBN). Time then was great in 1996. The environment was friendly, and everyone was busy doing one thing or the other. I guessed it was so exciting being

3

with the people you love. My Dad took very care of the family, providing us with all life expected from us at a time.

Lest I forget, I remember the chief security officer to EZE One Thousand was taking us to school in his car, and he decided to have a stopover at the residence of one of the richest men in Enugu close to the government residential area. Guess what I saw? I was curious and innovative and always wanted to know everything as a child. I amazingly discovered that the cars were packed on the topmost floor of the house. It was the scariest and most surprising thing I have ever seen. I wondered what kind of man owned such a house who decided to pack his cars in such a place. In my heart, I can vividly remember what I said to myself that one day I would become wealthy to own such a big house.

Unfortunately, for me, those thought was wishes that require processing and tremendous experiences to actualize such feats. Also, I remember fetching water at the stream daily for household use. The name of the stream is Miri Ocha. The word in English is white water. I enjoyed visiting the stream because it allows for swimming and playing with my friends. Close to the creek was a beautiful house built with bricks and owned by a wealthy family. One of the family members enjoyed talking with me, and this developed the desire to work very hard to attain tremendous success in life. However, it never occurred to me that life was not the bed of roses and that one needed to face challenges in life to succeed. Honestly, I admired the building and respected the family at that age.

However, I am always ready to go to school each weekday because some money will always be given to me to buy puff puffs. It was my usual delicacy at any time in school. I enjoyed it myself with friends. My mates gave me so much respect because of my strength and knowledge of Karate. So, I always enjoyed the company of my mates. Also, I was brilliant with all the subjects. Unfortunately, I was very stubborn and always wanted things done the way I wanted them.

One of the memorable incidents that happened to me as a child, in Enugu that I will not forget so quickly was the day the headteacher invited my father. What happened? I had a friend stealing his father's money and spending it on us in school. Unknown to me, I never realized the boy was stealing from the father's money and squandering it with us. So, one day the father discovered and wanted to know who was influencing the son to steal money. The boy told the parent that I was the one telling him to steal the money from him. The headteacher summoned all his friends, including the parent. Unfortunately, I was there too. That was a red day for me. The school invited my dad. Although, since I started schooling at Command Children's School. I have never been called for anything odd such as this. I denied the allegation from my friend. My friends and I were severely punished at school. In my most expansive imagination, thinking that the punishment was over, not knowing my dad had a different plan for me at home.

I got home that same day. I could not sit properly, considering the severity of my buttocks' pain, around midnight about going to the following day. My Dad woke me up and told me to follow him. He had already prepared a pepper to apply to my whole body. He did use the pepper on my buttock and my genitals. Then, he tied me to the center table of the living room. He severely lashed a good number of strokes. I cried profusely, but no one came to rescue me. Since that day, I have become very calm in school and avoided all my usual friends. My Dad brought out the best in me. I became serious with my life and always avoided occasions of trouble.

Subsequently, moving on to Abuja to start secondary school in 1999. There was great excitement because of my progress. Then one day, we had an English class that very day. English happened to be my worst nightmare, but I tried my best to put all my attention into it. I was interested in knowing English, but it wasn't easy for me. The teacher that was taking the subject made it more difficult. So, I was not the only one in the class; I found it hard to crack. Also, on the same day the man was teaching, the man got offended by the student in the class and told everyone to kneel. At the same time, the man went outside to fetch the cane to flog the whole class. I quickly stood up to run out of the class, knowing how I hate being beaten.

Sadly, for me, while trying to escape from the class, behold, at the same time the man was walking in with a cane. I became confused and speechless. He asked me where I was going, and I quickly told him that I wanted to ease myself. He was furious and gave me a very dirty slap. My head could not contain such a slap, and I quickly returned to my position.

However, I had a spectacular score in mathematics that has never been recorded in my school. Surprisingly, initially, I was not very good at maths, but I was interested in knowing it. Fortunately, I met a friend named Haruna, who ignited my interest and motivated me in maths. So, I decided to learn maths from him. He was patient in teaching me mathematics in JSS2, and I picked up significantly. I became very good at maths in JSS3. I became the best student in mathematics in the entire school. It led me to represent my school in different competitions, such as the cowbell mathematics competition. Lest I forget, In SSS3, I scored 100% in mathematics at maths. I had in my maths assessment 30% and all together culminated to an excellent score at maths which has never been recorded in my school. Secondary school was so interesting. I had the desire to become either a doctor or an engineer.

Eventually, I gained admission to Madonna University to study Medicine and Surgery. I started my 100 level with solid enthusiasm and successfully passed the pre-medical school into 200 level, which was competitive at the time. My mum bought me all the medical textbooks I needed for my onward study. 200 level was exciting because I started studying physiology, anatomy, and biochemistry and was about to start cadaver training. At one point, after visiting a certain mass conducted by Father Jude Okeosisi, my life completely changed. He said categorically on that mass that there is a student here who initially came here to study Medicine and Surgery, but you are supposed to be studying Engineering. So, my head tumbled, and I had never had rest since that very day. Also, I was infected for the very first time with a disease known as chickenpox. This made me leave the campus for my home in Abuja. I got home met my mum and told her that I would no longer be studying medicine and surgery and that I would like to change to engineering. My mum was shocked and asked why now; then I told her that the school fees were expensive and that I wouldn't want her to go through the stress of paying throughout my medical career. She became disturbed and said I shouldn't worry myself so much, that I should keep studying that she would handle it.

However, I insisted that I change to Engineering because the school fee for Medicine and Surgery will eventually increase as it progresses to other levels. My mum was seriously concerned about me and wanted the best for me. So, she decided to see her pastor to enquire if she should change. Later I told her that it was a message from God to me to switch to Engineering. Also, her pastor told her to leave me so that I could continue with my plans. My mum is a great woman and loves the things of God dearly. She always wanted the best for her children, and she taught all my siblings, including me, how to trust and rely on God for everything we do. She came home that day to confirm the message I heard from Father Jude. After she accepted, I had an intense relief and conviction to pursue my dreams with great joy.

Going to the University, I went to the registrar, picked up a change of course form, and filled it out. After filling out the record, I took the form to the engineering faculty. I got to the door of the head of the department for Electrical, and electronic engineering. With panic in my heart, something came on me and told me to knock and open the door. Knocking on the door, I was asked to come in by the HOD. I walked in and said to him that I wanted a change of course from medicine and surgery to engineering. He responded that I should go to chemical engineering or civil engineering, that the Electrical Electronic engineering was already filled up. I thanked him and proceeded to the chemical engineering department to meet the head of the department. On meeting the head of the department for Chemical engineering, he was shocked and earnestly cautioned me why I should make such a change on earth because it was unusual. Suddenly, he changed his mind and said I should get the form for him to sign. I was shocked, and I knew that God was responsible for the sudden change in men. He handed the signed form and handed it over to me without hesitation. I got to the hostel and was very happy that God saw me through. However, it was still not so easy on my side because I started receiving severe spiritual attacks in dreams and physically.

Nevertheless, I was not too troubled because I knew God was behind my decision. I had more trust in the Lord for His promises. I had to drop all the medical books aside, pick up engineering maths and chemical engineering textbooks and started studying them.

Although it was not easy, I kept matching with God's grace. Not surprisingly, my mate began to ask me why I had to change my course where I was doing well. I told them that God told me to change, and they began to make jest of me, but I never cared because I knew God was behind it. I studied very hard in Chemical Engineering to emerge with an excellent grade. Though it was difficult and stressful, I pulled through without hindrance. I would want to encourage anyone who read about my story, that if you are going through any challenge that you think is overwhelming, don't give up. Put your trust in God. He must surely see you through. I would recommend you stay with people who will encourage you and share the little they have with you. This kind of person should always be around you, look for them, and I promise you there will be no regret in the end. Also, remember that prayer is the key to having great success in life as a Christian. You don't necessarily have to be perfect, but no one who has put his/her hope in God came out defeated or disappointed.

Like my mentor would always say, "pray as if everything depends on prayers and work as if everything depends on you" quite a great quote from the Prophet of God (T. B Joshua).

Back to the story, I did my internship at Innoson plastic, where I learned the process of manufacturing plastics and tires for vehicles. It was a worthwhile experience because I met with its owner, and we became friends. He promised to offer me a job at his company when I finish my studies. On completing my Bachelor of Engineering, I decided to work with my mentor, Mr. Martin Anagboso. A great man with a caring heart. He took me as his biological son and gave me everything I needed. I worked for him for a few years and eventually served my country under the National Youth Service Corps in Bayelsa state. This is one of the oil and gas-producing states in my country, Nigeria.

In Bayelsa, I discovered that my nation was richly blessed and wondered why we were not seeing it at a time. My primary interest was to finish my service successfully and move on with life. I did my primary assignment in a small, lovely community called Epebu in Ogbia's local government area. The people were welcoming and entertaining. All the coopers were so happy that they came to such a community. I began to ask questions about the community, so they told me that a past crisis ravaged the community with another community called Nnembe, a neighboring community. I ask why? They replied, saying it was because of the oil in the ground. Both communities were dragging ownership of the land where oil was discovered. This caused a lot of death in the community.

I became scared, but something in me said, don't worry, God brought you here. Be calm! So, I began to think of how I could solve the problem by uniting people back into the community again. They seem not to be working together. My fellow coopers and I discussed this. We resolve that we will organize events such as games, dramas, beauty shows, singing competitions, etc., to return the community to what it used to be. On my own, I decided to join them most evenings to play football to understand them and relate well with them. They were such a lovely set of people who were ready to work with you to achieve a great result. This made me know their chiefs and older men in the community.

Approaching the end of our program, we implemented the unification program. The entire community was so happy and commended us for organizing such a program that brought them together as one loving community. They were amazed by our ingenuity. I was thrilled that I was able to achieve that for the community.

Another spectacular event happened; on a certain night, criminals attacked the community with guns. They were firing gun bullets in the air inside the community to disperse obstructors. Also, they had plans to carry one of the new speed boats in the community. One of the coopers, Alex, rushed into my room to take cover. So, I told Alex to keep himself very low for the criminals not to see him. Eventually, they were repelled by the community vigilante group, who ran after them on another speed boat to take back their boat. It was a terrific experience but thank God for everything because everything later became calm and settled. One of the vigilante members later told me that the community felt it was kidnapers who came to take the coopers who were lodged in the community, and that was why they came to check if we were safe. Apart from that incident, everything was great and exciting in the community.

Sincerely, I will not forget the community in my entire life. I have plans to visit the community to help them in the future.

In 2013, my service ended. Following that, I began my job search. I looked for a job for months and had no results. So, I decided to travel to the United Arab Emirates with a tourist visa, searching for a job. I spent three months looking for work but was unsuccessful. My three-month visa to the United Arab Emirates ultimately expired. I had no other option than to return to my country, Nigeria. It was disappointing because my aim was not actualized. I kept hope alive and had complete trust in God.

However, while I was in the UAE, I met someone who owned a security company. The name of the company is known as Alread Security LLC. He promised to assist me in finding a security position. I was skeptical at first and never believed the man would follow through on his promise, but I continued to trust God for guidance and breakthrough. The man eventually followed through on his promise and provided me with a two-year security guard contract in the UAE. It was one of the happiest times of my life. After finishing my two-year employment contract under challenging circumstances, I left the company mysteriously for Nigeria. To date, I am still wondering how I managed to leave the country still alive on earth. I had terrible experiences in the UAE. One of those encounters was the terrible dreams I had. I was nearly killed (Kept secret) in the UAE, but Jesus protected me and made me leave the country. Lest I forget, one astonishing thing happened to me, I had a dream which revealed my prophetic picture. God showed me that I would become a great leader, and others would bow down to me. God kept telling great things for the time being.

Another one happened when I was on my duty one night on patrol. I saw a few gatherings of young boys outside the free zone. So, I was not comfortable with them being around such a place. I had to use my touch to put a flash of light on them, and I took cover, so they won't see me. They noticed immediately and began to spin their car in vexation that someone had seen them. I had to quickly run as I could, then called the police about the incident. Apart from all these dilemmas, UAE was a wonderful place to visit and spend with family and friends.

The terrifying thing that happened to me in UAE was when all the money saved in the United Arab Emirates (UAE) was taken at the airport. I got confused at the airport and was strongly devastated. I started hearing strange voices that made me act odd at the airport. I was picked up by the police and locked up in a cell with a handcuff. I have never experienced this kind of incident in my life before. My whole life came to a stop, and I wondered what had happened to me. God was with me in that cell. Eventually, I was released and sent to the boarding area. Again, the strange voice returned, and I started acting odd at the airport. Orders were given to me, and I took those orders unconsciously without realizing what was wrong with me. Till I got into the airplane, I moved to Kigali en route to Lagos state Nigeria. I could not fathom what was wrong with me. It was an intense spiritual attack coming from the UAE.

Amazingly, God was still with me on the plane. I felt the plane would explode because of what I was hearing. It stopped, and when we got to Kigali, I began to act strangely again, and I was handcuffed the second time on the plane. So, they brought me down, told me to descend the aircraft, and took me to a room where they removed the handcuff. Then, I became very calm till I got to Lagos state Nigeria airport. I got to Nigeria thinking that the attack was over, another strange voice came at the airport, and I became scared again. I started taking command from anonymous voices. I was later arrested by an immigration officer who held my passport, and while this was happening, I forgot to take my luggage. The immigration took me to their office and told me to sit down. I was told the UAE official at the airport said I was deported, but this was not true. They lied. Possibly to avoid any unforeseen trouble. I knew I was innocent on my path because I finished my job with the security company and left them successfully without a problem. Anyway, I kept putting my trust in God and was focused.

On the other hand, I was devastated. So, when I got home

to Abuja to meet my wailing mother, who kept vigil for me to ensure that I was safe. Sadly, the worst was that I had nothing to fall back on because all the money I saved from the security company in UAE was collected at the airport. I had to start from the beginning again, searching for a way to survive. Regrettably, I saw myself as a failure and wondered what people would say about my ordeal because I was the only person that knew what I was going through. I had nobody to explain what transpired in UAE. Only my poor mother understood and began to take me from one prayer house to another. She kept praying for me. Another strange thing started to happen in our place at Mararaba in Nasarawa state.

Again, the strange voice returned, and the worst began to happen in my house. This spiritual attack was something I don't pray my enemy to encounter. **Wherever the attack was coming from, I believe they wanted me dead, but God disagreed because there was a more extraordinary assignment, he wanted me to fulfill in the future. Thank God for my precious mother, who stood by me in my prayers.** She kept praying for me to come out of it. She knew they wanted to kill me. Above all, I kept being strong because of the support from my family. I became very slim; then, my mum took off the only cloth I came home with and handed me another fabric. Till today she has not told me where she kept that cloth. Also, I kept hearing strange voices and later became sick for more than a month in a national hospital in Abuja. My family stood behind me and paid all the bills that were incurred. Food was provided, and I was unaware of who provided them until now; That reminds me, I would ask my mother.

Indeed, it was a trying time for me. In my whole life, I have never experienced such a thing. I wanted the very best, and most importantly, I wanted to be very successful. Satan knew this and kept attacking me from all corners. Moreover, I began to lose confidence in God, and my prayer life began to dwindle. God allowed it.

Discharged from the hospital, coming home to Mararaba, again I began to think about my journey and my process. I wondered why my life turned out this way. I obeyed my parent and did everything a reasonable child would do to succeed, yet vicissitudes were all around. I remembered this adage that says thus, "Uneasy lies the head that wears the crown" what a quote. However, there was nothing I could do to change the situation. But I kept thinking. My mum encouraged me to be strong and that life is sometimes like that. I felt elated a bit, but inside I was burning. I traveled at first to change my parent's life, but it turned out to be a disappointment. I felt nobody understood what I went through, but I was confident God understood.

The only option I had was to start staying with my younger brother, Ebuka, managing one of my mum's shops at Wuse zone 4 in Abuja. On progressing further, I started serving in the restaurant, helping to clean, wash, and dispatch food to customers at the bank closer to the shop. I would trek and distribute food to the customer. My brother was very hard working and had great ingenuity for business. We worked together, and I helped him out with most activities. Yet, I was not happy and satisfied with my life. I got hold of my laptop, and something in me said, why not start looking for a school specializing in oil and gas engineering? I got one school at Aberdeen called Robert Gordon University. Again, the same voice said the search for the agent responsible for the University in Nigeria. This time I believe this voice was from God. No doubt. I contacted the agent, and the agent responded very well; she briefed me about the process of admission to Robert Gordon University. At that moment, I had not any money, but surprisingly I was not worried. Another voice came again and said send a mail to your uncle in the United State of America and tell him about your plans. I did it, and God perfected it to the letter.

In 2017, my admission process to Robert Gordon University

to study Oil and gas engineering began to materialize. It was the hand of God. I could not believe it. All I had to do was keep thanking God and saying my prayers. My Dad eventually came to Abuja to help in the process. My uncle agreed to pay my fees and sponsor my journey to the United Kingdom. He did something that I would never forget for the rest of my life. My Uncle, Dr. Tochukwu, exemplified what most uncles cannot do for their nephews. He spent more than 30000 pounds on my process. I owe him great things in the future. He is truly a great man indeed! One issue came up along the process about a bank statement. It was as if that would stop the process. That same voice said, " Go and meet your mentor and explain your problem to him. I did precisely that, and it turned out positive. He agreed to help me and kept #5,000 000. 00 in my bank account for 28 days for me to print a bank statement. This bank statement was meant for the United Kingdom Embassy in Abuja. Later I filed for an appointment at the embassy, and an interview date was fixed. I went out very early for the interview with great enthusiasm. I went into the embassy and made my document submission. I was told to come the next day to pick up my passport. Then, I went back home and kept praying because I knew that only God could see me through, considering how one feels about what goes on in Nigeria. Regardless, God did it. My passport came out, and the UK visa was stamped on it. I was pleased and excited that I was going out of the country again to make my parents and family proud. On a serious note, I was the happiest man on the earth's surface. Considering my kind of person, I knew Nigeria was not where I could work and have rest of mind. I have always wanted to leave the country for something better. Gladly, God made it possible. I was coming to meet my family. They were all happy for me and celebrated with me. My mum said it was God's time. Mum kept praying for me as usual.

Finally, the day came for me to leave Nigeria for the UK. It was like I should stay one more day in Nigeria, but on the other hand, I had to leave the country to pursue my dreams and aspirations. My brother, Dad, and I drove that morning to the Nnamdi International Airport in Abuja. Everyone was excited and joyful that I was finally leaving the country for good to pursue what would supposedly change my life. On our way, the car halted at the road to Asokoro bridge at Abuja. No one could tell the cause of the vehicle stop. Although I panicked a little because of the delay, this could cause my journey. My brother came out of the vehicle and opened the vehicle's bonnet to discover that something had gone wrong. He checked the radiator and the battery head to ensure stability. Luckily, he was able to put on the ignition, and it hummed, and eventually, we again continued the road to the airport. We successfully got to the airport and began to think if I should stay one more day, but this was not possible because all travel arrangements had been concluded and decided. I began to miss my family again, especially my brother, whom I respect because of his human nature and great spirit. He always inspires me. His story is one every aspiring entrepreneur should listen to or read about. I bid them farewell and embraced my brother and Dad. Then, my dad said something I will not forget in a hurry: I should remember the family I came from, work hard, and hard work does not kill. This word resonated daily in my life and all activities. Thank God for my dad. My Dad remains my mentor, his experience in life gave me hope that more beautiful days are ahead of me. He kept saying that the place he could not get to that I would get there. Growing up, I know that success requires hard work and perseverance, most notably putting my trust in God daily for His lead. Now, let's continue; I said goodbye to them, and finally my dad said in my language, IGBO …. Ji si ike….. this means well done and keep working hard. I went to the airport, checked in my luggage, and went onwards to board my ticket. I was so happy now that I was traveling again out of Nigeria for good to see the other side of the world. With so many goals written and on my mind.

Appreciating my uncle in my heart, who gave me such a tremendous opportunity to succeed in a foreign land. I would forever be grateful to him for such a vast opportunity he availed me to change the course of my life and destiny. My uncle is a man of few words, intelligent, and the humblest person I have come to know on this planet. He is Gem! I passed the security checks without hassles and sat down on the lounge, waiting to hear my boarding time. 8 am sharp! We were called to start boarding. I stood up and joined the cue at once and eventually entered the plane and quickly located my sit and took my sitting position. I thanked God once again for allowing me to embark on another journey after my ordeals and challenges in life, especially in UAE. It can only be God. No one could have possibly done this.

The final boarding was now made, and it took another 5mins for the plane to leave Abuja, Nigeria. I finally said goodbye to Nigeria. In my mind, I knew that this was God's time for me to put perspectives right and change the course of my life and destiny. Thank God for my family, who stood by me at my low ebb moments. Such a fantastic family! I don't know what I would have done without them. On the plane, I watched a few entertainments and movies on display. We got to London, and we got a connecting flight to Aberdeen that evening, the same day. We all descended from the plane and instantly knew I was in a different climatic zone because of the intense cold. I loved it and thanked God. I saw my university representative already waiting to take me to my hostel at Robert Gordon University Scotland. What a great joy for me and the happiness this brought to my bones. Unknown that I was in for another very challenging moment in my life. Regardless, with renewed hope and desire to learn all I could to succeed in my academics. Vigour and hope for a better tomorrow radiate around me.

Furthermore, classes began, and I engulfed myself with every level of seriousness in my academics. This yielded fruits but not as anticipated, but God was involved. An astonishing thing happened: I worked so hard for one course, business essentials. I got a D on it. This did not go well with me, but I never gave up. However, I kept encouraging myself. After that, I went into the second semester and held at the same pace. My worst nightmare came when the engineering school said I could not continue with my dissertation because of my grade on a course, environmental engineering. I was mad about this. Although, I never saw what God was doing. I became worried. God used that situation to keep me in Aberdeen in Scotland till date.

Most importantly, He used it to shape me better for a more excellent assignment he had planned. I continued to pray and trusted the almighty God. Indeed, he said something about my situation, but I did not listen. I drafted a letter to the engineering school to consider my plea and remark on the course because this could be a mistake. All efforts proved abortive. Relentlessly, I wrote the second letter, telling them to consider my plea on the grounds of my dyslexic symptoms. They honored and remarked on it and eventually discovered that I did not fail the course. By then, my mate had already graduated and left Aberdeen because their visa was due to expire in January 2020. Finally, I heard from the panel presiding over my case in December 2019. The university immigration agreed to extend my visa for another 6 to 7 months. This gladdened my heart because God was busy working things out in His way. Poor me, I could not see clearly in the spirit realm to know that God was not silent in my case. I had to reach out to my family about it. However, they were not happy about it. Hence, they kept praying for me to succeed in all I do. Mainly, my mum stood in daily praying about my circumstances. She kept encouraging me that God was with me and that I should not worry. This I eventually realized that God knew all I was going through. If you have failed and you felt you have lost everything, take inspiration from the quote of Dr. A. P. J Abdul Kalam about Life, "If you fail, never give up because F.A.I.L. means "first Attempt in Learning"; End is not the end. E.N.D. means "Effort

Never Dies"; If you get No as an answer, remember N.O. means "Next Opportunity." So, be positive.

My visa was extended, and I completed my dissertation with ease and badged with MSc in Oil and Gas Engineering from Robert Gordon University in July 2020. After my dissertation, I had another strange experience that I would not want my worst enemy to go through. I had a spiritual attack. It was as if my heart wanted to come out of my mouth, which made me restless. I was taken to the hospital the same day, and when I got to the hospital, I was told nothing was wrong with me. I was surprised because I was not ok. Eventually, I got discharged and got home, thinking that was the end. Another one struck again; this time, I heard voices as I experienced in Dubai. I had to come out of my house deserted and confused. I believe someone called the police, and they took me to the hospital. Now, I was admitted to the hospital for more than a month. I began to experience even more spiritual arrows hitting from all corners. I kept my trust and hope in God. He was the only one that would help me. The doctors seemed not to understand what I was going through.

Later, I began to get back myself, and, going further, I was finally discharged to go to my house. When I got home at 10c Justice Street, I could not understand the place. The worst one was that the coronavirus was at its peak, and everybody seemed to be in their home with families or possibly alone. Overall, I appreciated God for seeing me through this ordeal. This was part of what inspired my story. So, I felt I needed to share it with young people to learn from them and put their situation to God for all their worst nightmares and challenges facing us as young people. As young people, we want to be successful, but God takes us through an extraordinary journey to birth the new man in us, becoming change agents in our communities and the world.

Now at home, thinking about what the next move and direction were. I thought of finishing my job and leaving for Nigeria to go ahead and start managing my little poultry business with some money left in my account. My cousin, Abuchi, suggested we should go to America, but on second thought, the lockdown or pandemic in America restricted visitors from traveling. So, Abuchi came up with a plan B to carry on with another master's program at RGU. He said he had plans to study international marketing management. Although I was initially skeptical of the whole new idea, I eventually saw reasons for his opinion. He applied first, and I followed suit. Then, after the application. We had to wait for the University's feedback. This took more than two weeks. However, they sent us a message regarding our application to answer a few immigration questions about why we wanted to study another course at RGU. We gave them the answers we felt were convincing enough to earn us that path.

As the days progressed, they sent me a mail saying that I was successful and could go ahead to pay my fees. Surprisingly, my cousin was not granted admission into International Marketing Management. The reason is that while Abuchi was applying, he mistakenly put international business instead of International Marketing Management. He did use it the second time and got the course on global business management. He saw it so strange, but I knew that was how God wanted it to happen in my heart. It was divinely arranged and orchestrated.

Another challenge came: the statement of account that needed to be kept in my account for 28 days. So, both of us needed more than £12000 each in our respective accounts for at least a month to present to the home office in the UK. My cousin eventually saw someone who agreed to give him some money to keep in his account because he would pay interest on the agreed sum. He decided and collected the money. Mine was not forthcoming. My uncle decided to give me £2000, which I added. Also, a great friend, Mr. Chimaroke, handed me over £5000. The money I contributed was added to my account for 30 days. After 30 days, I returned all their money. Of course, I thanked them and appreciated their gestures. This is important! Again, something came up from the University that I must exit the country because my visa had expired. I could not go because there was a restriction in the whole UK. I gave them this reason, but they insisted that the CAS (Confirmation of Acceptance to Study) would not be given to me. Well, I kept trusting God to see me through. Still, I took the initiative to do what I could personally do to change the situation. I drafted a letter to UK immigration regarding my case, and they replied and gave me a special assurance letter to cover my onward stay in the UK. Therefore, I gave this letter to the University, and they told me that they still stand in their former position. Now, I knew I had to pray hard this time. I decided to call a prayer line of SCOAN (Synagogue Church of All Nation) to establish my circumstances. I realized I needed more prayers from my partners to commit my ways after their prayers and encouragement. I had a conviction in me that God was involved in my situation. **Every** worry that seemed to trouble me left instantly. Therefore, I made up my mind that whatever comes that I would take it in good faith with thanksgiving in my heart. What a joy knowing GOD! He is reliable. Like the saying, when God is with you, everything falls in pleasant places for your sake. Even the laws of the land will be changed for your sake. This is true! I experienced it. The UK immigration promulgated a law that if you have spent more than one year in the UK studying, you do not need a statement of account from any bank. Another striking law introduced by the UK government was that you don't require a tuberculosis test result before applying for your visa if you are in the UK already. I tried to ask for my CAS letter for my visa based on the laws. Even at that, the school rejected my request. They told me to return to my country, and on getting home, I should call and send them my stamped passport from immigration officials. So, after then, they can decide what to do for me.

However, I never gave up. Like the saying goes from the Quote of Joseph Campbell "Where you stumble and fall, there you will find gold." My initial exceptional assurance offered by the home office was about to elapse, yet my aim was not accomplished. What next did I do? I applied yet again, telling UK home office to give me additional time to finish my student application process. Luckily, they gave me another special assurance letter. I was thrilled. God was at work. God remains faithful. Meanwhile, all these issues were happening to me while my brother had already started lectures without restrictions. I never bothered because I knew God was at work in my life.

Unfortunately, I lost my only part-time job as a cleaner. This means I had no money to buy food or life necessities. Still, I wasn't worried because I knew it would come and go. This was the complete trust I had in God. I decided to book my ticket to return to my country, Nigeria. Too, I felt the school wanted me to go home. I had to discuss it with a friend, and he advised that I should return to Nigeria, then come back. After I had booked my ticket, I sent the itinerary to the University, and they acknowledged it. Also, they told me that once I got home, I should send the stamped ticket on my passport to them as evidence that I was back in Nigeria. This confirmed what I had in my heart: I would finally be heading back to Nigeria. I told my parents about the situation, and they had no other alternative than to go with my suggestions. In all this, God was still working things out for me. My ticket had already been rescheduled three (3) times by British airways because of Covid-19.

Furthermore, in my heart, God was on top of the situation. Here was December 2020; the school had already closed. My ticket says the first week of January 2021 was when I would leave the UK. On Christmas day, I was so happy with myself and decided to visit my friend, Chimaroke, to spend time and celebrate with his family. All worries left me because I knew that was the way God works. Therefore, I decided always to thank Him in whatever situation. Encourage yourself in a difficult situation, and I recommend staying close to people who encourage you.

Most significantly, stay connected to a Christian channel that would speak to your situation and remain through to praying for you. What I did was stay connected to Emmanuel tv. I got encouragement from my mentor, Senior Prophet T. B. Joshua. A great man whose legacy lives on! He was such a great inspiration to me. I call him my father.

Something happened that shocked me about God. The school contacted me in the first week of January 2021, and they have decided to issue me my CAS letter, which means I can now apply in the UK. All this happened after having submitted different letters to the University to allow me to complete my application in the UK. Indeed, I was surprised by the entire situation. However, I knew God was behind all that. Also, British airways have rescheduled my ticket 4xs now. I decided to ask for a refund with all this happening, and I eventually got a full refund. It was a great joy that God walked with me in all situations. RGU gave me the CAS as they promised, and I quickly borrowed some money from a friend, Chimaroke, and I applied within the UK. In the same week, a positive response came from UK immigration that I was successful with my application. In all, I was grateful to God and my partners in prayers. Immediately, I resumed classes as a student of international marketing management. Now, in a new course which was different from Engineering. I decided I would work very hard and kept trusting in God in every situation that came my way. So far, God has been faithful. Miraculously I got back my former part-time job because I had some bills and school fees to pay. God was so kind. This friend, Odion, got an appointment with an engineering firm that also assisted with some money to pay part of my fees. He stood by me at my worst moment. A great friend indeed!

In my undergraduate, I studied chemical Engineering and Health, safety, and the environment with a company affiliated with SHELL. Also, I did security training where I was trained by Dubai police and Australian security firms as a private security guard and obtained my PSBD license. In my master's, I did Oil and Gas Engineering and international marketing management at RGU. I would want to encourage someone who is performing poorly in his/her academics not to give up but to continue to study hard. **The table will turn right if consistency becomes your roadmap. Take encouragement from my story and be strong. Now, I have successfully graduated in MSc. oil and gas, MSc. International marketing with distinction. Also, I have received different awards coming from VSA recognizing my contribution towards designing an application to help social workers to deliver efficient services to their client with ease, three (3) innovation certificates and recognition from the Wood company for diversity and inclusion. As you have read, God has been faithful and gracious to me.**

Now in business, as a social entrepreneur in Alovea working on changing the lives of vulnerable children, supporting healthy living and well-being of people. This is inspiring because my experience in medical school has made me realize how important I wanted people's well-being to stay top-notch.

Aha", Ouch. Honestly, I had some terrifying experiences and moments as a Christian in my spiritual faith journey. Just as Joseph was purified through pain, this was the same thing I went through. I began to ask myself if it was because my name was Joseph. Although, I did not have any reply whatsoever. I never mind because the realization that God was supporting my position gave me rest and assurance of hope for the future. Salvation is a process. However, you can be Christian yet not salvaged. Hence, God qualifies our salvation journey. God takes us through the wilderness to test and mature us in our journey. Therefore, he said we should work for our salvation with fear and trembling (Philippians 2:12). Paul knew that going to church does not qualify you for salvation. Instead, he values the journey and excellent processing than the result. I had that complete understanding of this fact. It does not mean you earn salvation, but this is a journey you walk through with HIM. Trust me; He knows all our challenges even when it seems He is not saying anything. He is still there doing something outstanding in your life. Nothing ever surprises God, but this can trouble us because of our limitations as humans. He wants to walk us through whatever life offers us in our journey and processes in life. Would you let Him? Reflect on this.

Now you may ask, who am I? Yes! My name is Joseph Azubuike Uzodinma Onyekwuluje. He was a young lad who God captured at his lowest ebb, undeserving of anything by my past circumstances. Jesus Christ saw a different person with a passion for serving Him; I knew that God was watching all my activities, although I might not have been convinced. Profound revelation from the scripture gave me a deep dimension of God's presence in our world today. With what we are seeing in the world today, so many people are ignorant that God is aware of our situations. Looking closer at what we see around us, how do you view your circumstances? What do you see as a Christian? From my perspective, God is telling us something, especially in remembering the less privileged and the weak in our society, the disadvantaged, the have-nots, and the strong who probably lack the wisdom to make meaning out of their lives. However, many might argue that it was a mistake from man due to negligence and exploitation. I would agree. Take note, every one of us sees lives differently with varied opinions. The government of every nation must recognize the challenge its people face and prioritize their goals according to the scale of preference to better the situation of lives. It is lacking in some nations, and it will be wise to address this to solve imminent dangers lurking around which erupt their ugly head to cause poverty. Like My mentor, Senior Prophet T. B. Joshua, said I quote "Nothing can keep us together as one than the deep love for God and humanity."

My experiences with my father in heaven and the blessing He bestowed on me from the word of God.

He blessed my hand just as He said in his word in Genesis 49: 22 Joseph is a fruitful bough, even a fruitful bough by a well; whose branches run over the wall. However, the archers have sorely grieved him and shot at him, and hated him: but his bow abode in strength and the arms of his hands were made strong by the hands of the mighty God of Jacob: from thence is the shepherd, the stone of Israel:) 25 Even by the God, the father who shall bless thee with the blessings of heaven above, blessings of the deep that Leith under, blessings of the breast, and the womb. 26. The blessing of the father have prevailed above the blessing of my progenitors unto the utmost bound of the everlasting hills: They shall be on the head of Joseph, and on the crown of the head of him that was separated from his brethren.

Our Lord made a promise to me in Deuteronomy 33: 13, He said And of Joseph, Blessed of the Lord be his Land with the precious things of heaven, with dew, and the deep lying beneath. And with the precious fruits brought forth by the sun and with the precious things put forth by the moon. And with the chief things of the mountains, and with the precious things of the earth and the fullness thereof and the goodwill of him that dwelt in the bush. From the verse Genesis 49: 26, God said let the blessing come upon the head of Joseph and upon the top of the head of him, that was separated from his brethren. His glory is like the firstling of his bullock and his horn of a wild. OX: with them, he shall push the people and together to the ends of the earth: and they are ten thousand of Ephraim and they are the thousands of Manasseh.

Lest I forget I went through 5 coats of mystery spiritually, firstly, coat of archers, this was from unknown and known people. They hurt me so badly, but I kept on my journey knowing fully well they would come back to seek my help. Secondly, I went through the coat of son given by my father while wearing it displayed uniqueness and developed my character. Thirdly, I experienced the coat of a servant during my teenage years as a student in secondary school and university days. The coat of sacrifice was experienced after university days out with Nigeria in the UAE and Scotland. Lastly going through the coat of sovereign in a mysterious way only God can explain. This last one showed me that God put his children in a position where we must trust him, and he has a purpose in every lesson He teaches us.

Simple Lessons learned from my past (Story)
Some of the lessons learned along my journey,

1. Let your journey or experience inspire you daily
2. Be simple and yet be ready for the unknown
3. Prayer is very key to your journey as a Christian
4. Learn new skills, you don't necessarily have to work in the area where you studied in the university
5. Be apt to learn new leaps and challenges that come up
6. Seek a mentor who resonates with your experiences
7. humility
8. Speak out about the things you don't like.
9. List your strengths, weaknesses, opportunities, and threats before or lie ahead of you.
10. Learn to save money that comes along your way because money can sometimes be equated to a child if properly nurtured can grow and eventually be used for something useful
11. Read books that resonate with your experiences.
12. Respect those that come along your journey and appreciate them. Also, remember them when things eventually become ok with you.
13. Appreciate your journey and be joyful while going through your ordeals

14. Be sure not to compare yourself with others because everyone has his roadmap

15. Enjoy every moment of it

16. Avoid complicated life and situation around you.

17. Always remember that no exact rule to life, take each day slowly as it comes and become more aware of who you are.

18. Waite patiently for your own time to come and adapt to situations that come but always remember your goals and dreams.

19. Avoid being afraid to make mistakes, remember everyone makes mistakes because perfection eludes all.

20. Be optimistic for the future and trust God to accomplish His promises.

21. Love others, even those who do not like you.

22. Learn to save money to avoid unforeseen events that you might not cope with.

2

PRESENT

What are the problems you are solving? Yes, from my end, working hard to change the bad that I see that causes problems for others. My desire to help the weak, poor, disadvantaged, and strong is my core desire as I keep offering my part to society through my partners. Also, I desire to do even more, such as building homes for people that they can call home, using the product I sell to improve individual's lives, and making a difference in my world as God permits. Using gifts like the interpretation of dreams, prophecy, writing skills, and knowledge to assist those God allows me to change or impact their lives meaningfully.

As a social entrepreneur with ALOVEA, an ASEA associate, aspiring author of Joseph processing, Joseph tears, You, faith journey, innovator, and transformational agent. In my journey, I came across the book called "The Joseph Calling." I am grateful to Os Hillman for founding the Change Agent Master Mentor Program. It was a fantastic curriculum that changed my perception and gave me more insight into my journey and process. Also, I have decided to work with some reputable organizations to champion this excellent assignment, such as the Synagogue Church of All Nations (SCOAN), ALOVEA, and the Change Agent Master Mentor Program (CAMMP). I am also looking forward to other organizations as the Holy Spirit leads. I encourage the readers of this piece to partner with great organizations whose inspiration is in their area to discover their real value fully.

The challenges I faced in my life as a teenager in Enugu (Nigeria), Abuja (Nigeria), United Arab Emirates (UAE), and Scotland (United Kingdom) prepared me for a more extraordinary dimension of what I am to face in the future. Don't get carried away! I am still being processed and fashioned the way God wants me to be. Education was an eye-opener; it gave me perseverance, knowledge, and an eye-opener to world politics and its environs. My spiritual battle gave me a revelation on how God prepares his servants or leaders for critical assignments. Walking in the spirit is so beautiful and exciting (Paul's affirmation). When you genuinely walk in a relationship with God, you begin to seek an opinion from God and not from man. He keeps directing you on the path he wants you to go.

In my relationships, people tend to misunderstand my opinion because when you are where God wants you to be, Satan will do everything possible to sever your relationship with people there. One walking with God tends to overcome with love and carefulness.

In 2022 and beyond, the world will be like this, yes! It will become times entirely controlled by God. Christians faithful, Muslims, and other religions alike would begin to discover their identity properly. Christians might not have money in their pocket this does not necessarily mean he is not rich. He is rich because Christ has made him so. Taking reference from Genesis 39 verse 2, "the Lord told us that the Lord helped Joseph **become** a successful man" when he was still living in the house of his master, Potiphar the Egyptian. If we dive deep into this, this means someone can live physically without money in his hand, or own properties, cars, anything money can buy, yet the person is successful. Reading the scriptures slowly, repeatedly, attentively, and with forgiveness opens revelation to us. "Lord helped Joseph" means that Joseph could not help himself as such, and that is why God helped him. "Become" in Genesis 39 verse 2 implies a process. This means that God was in the process of making Joseph successful already; this means, that the success had been established. Always remember that the people with Joseph's anointing are generally broke in the eyes of men. Joseph's mantle will go through the church and world this season. Also, Joseph saw something others did not see (Exodus 13:19).

Joseph knew this, and he needed to be in the proper behavior or consistency to walk in this realm and blessing. This means in the year 2022 and beyond, God will begin to promote men who are in the stage of "become". People would recognize them and place them in positions that ordinary they don't deserve, but that is God's position. The unwitty invention would begin to emanate from these. Hidden mysteries unknown to men would come to light. When we start to hear this or that, it means Christ is near to us. As Christians, we should pursue excellence in all we do. Run with your goals and dreams God has given you and avoid envying someone else's achievements or accomplishments. Everyone on earth has been uniquely blessed in their ways. Support others and help them accomplish their goals too.

Another thing that Jesus Christ would bring "balance amongst Africans and White alike gradually and slowly" all around the world. It seems as if the people from the European nations, America, the United Kingdom, or western world, and other parts of the world seem to be more prosperous than the continent of Africans in the eyes of men. This is not true! God has blessed us equally, but that complete realization by Africans is still lacking now. This is the reason why God wants to bring a balance to this. It has been established! Nothing will stop it. It must surely come to pass! It has been decreed and signed by GOD! I cannot change it, and neither can you or anyone change it. Maybe I would have said let me dialogue with God for change, but my opinion does not matter here. That is, it! Let us get ready.

It is coming! Africa is becoming, but it still would not be easy to go just like that. Something must happen, and a journey to cross and come to that point we all desire as Africans or western world must take the approach of relying entirely on GOD who created the world and hard work that it requires to become a continent, we all want to see.

In Education, new inventions would be released uniquely; problems would be solved with research. Young people would make all manner of discoveries, and uncanny truths would be revealed. People would be rewarded accordingly, and when this time comes, you will know it is God and not man. Science and technology would apply but not wholly. Secrets behind some novel inventions would be revealed and uncovered. The fact remains that God would bring a "balance". God endorsed it, and I saw it clearly through dreams. No one can stop it, including me. This He has decreed. We should be ready! It is coming! It is the way of God. His nature has been revealed to Us in this generation. Do we deserve all this? Only Him can answer this. Unique ideas would come from a source that we least expect. Remember, God can use anyone. Takes note! We all are undeserving, so as believers we need to admit His word as a standard for our lives. I would encourage people to appreciate others and love everyone.

God will uniquely show His power through novel inventions in medicine; yes, drugs are excellent. Science and technology are fantastic. It provides opportunities for growth in any nation but still, God's power walking in the spirit would continue to be felt in the life of people because Jesus is the same yesterday, today, and forever. He does not change, but we certainly change as humans. God's word remains our standard. He speaks to us every day, but some hear, and some don't. New products would come out that would wow! Men. People would be so healthy and have sound minds as Christians. Surgeries would be performed remotely, liposuction would be done spiritually, human faces would be reconstructed, and bodies would be transformed by the holy spirit.

It is time God wants to reveal his glory ultimately. However, there are prices attached: faithfulness, hard work, consistency, prayers, reliance, trust, not expecting to be blessed, and true humility; the rest comes and is decided by God. Remember, we have not done anything to deserve salvation but a gift from God. Therefore, no one should boast about this thing. Notwithstanding, we still have a part to play as a people. Jesus Christ is the head of the spiritual kingdom and is aware of everything. Whether visible or invisible. God knows.

In some of my revelation about the churches, GOD will be raising Josephs across the 7 mountains of culture in the society, which includes governments, family (protection of family unit, values), religion, education, media, art and entertainment, economy (business world, science, and technology).

In relationships, people who did you wrong will be coming back to YOU. They will be afraid to repeat it because they are aware of what they did BUT that doesn't matter because YOUR response will let them know that there is a reason YOU were given that position. GOD also needs to trust YOU with the WEALTH of the land. The wealth of the mountain he has called you to serve (money, resources, tools, information, knowledge, food) to help the people during the famine (difficult times) and not sell it trying to make a profit for yourself.

ACTION PLAN

1. Continue to follow your passion and what comes to your heart
2. Sensitive to what happens around you
3. Remain consistent with saying my rosary or prayers
4. Continue with my writing and trading of my product
5. Continue to meet with new networks on my Rader

6. Remain consistent with my values, integrity, and respect for others

7. Follow my passion to succeed

8. Don't deny yourself of small indulgences or pleasures that enrich life. Remember, little indulgences are the way forward.

9. Control your finance and inculcate the habit of savings.

10. If you are married set aside some money for your unborn children and the ones already in existence.

11. Put down your vision and mission statement on paper and constantly review them to know if you are following them accordingly.

12. Set aside money for a gift, arms giving, and support loved ones because they are also your source of strength when the going gets tough.

13. Be responsible for your life and be disciplined.

14. Set aside money for old age because one cannot rely on the state or government, or family. If you have no old age plan, you will lose control of your level of comfort, style, and luxury, control of your financial freedom, lose control of bodily functions that lower your activities.

15. If you are in business, identify the wrong partners in business, strategize on a good business proposal, have a foothold on your business, value your best staff and give them the best to keep the business running smoothly on top, and ensure your premises are neat and formulate a good business logo

3

FUTURE

I will be doing the following: providing financial security for struggling families, ensuring families' next generation has access to educational opportunities no matter the cost, making philanthropic commitments that can benefit their community and country, and being an example to others. Also, that education and commitment will lead to a better life no matter where you start, solving humanity's problems such as poverty and unemployment silently as God permits me and gives me the opportunity, doing charity works, assisting farmers in all areas of agriculture, and setting up businesses to bring more significant opportunities in the life of others. I would also be helping families, establishing families to reach their potential, and opening new opportunities to enhance livelihood and sanity. In terms of inventions, I would introduce new products in the market that would significantly put smiles on the faces of families.

Above all, my complete trust goes to God almighty and who is the source of blessing to all humanity. Thank you, Lord!

I am encouraging my readers to look inward and not just pray alone. I mean, prayer is very crucial. We can solve many problems around us when we look inward and try to know what God is saying and use our gift of knowledge acquired from experiences and education to solve problems, man, faces.

Certainly, by adopting experiences and skills, solutions will emanate, and God will begin a new thing in our lives. Sincerity and openness among us are essential. Most critical is loving which we see beyond hatred, envy, jealousy, pride, etc. If we can do this, then change will come, and we can now have a good beginning in our life, careers, health, businesses, and all ramification of our lives.

My message to my readers is to acknowledge God, submit to His authority rather than ours, accept our mistakes, and forgive ourselves and those who hurt us badly. Like a mentor would always say that the person most injured by unforgiveness is you! And not the others who hurt you. However not easy, but it is worth doing. Therefore, knowing better would bring wisdom and grace to you. According to 2 Chronicle 7: 14, God said that if people called by my name would humble themselves and acknowledge their sins and ask for forgiveness genuinely, then Our Father in heaven would hear, show mercy, and heal their land. There are basic things to note; God wants us to realize 1. We all are called by His name, 2. Humility is critical, 3. Prayer is even more critical, 4. Acknowledging our wrongs because all have sinned and fallen short of God's glory, 5. Then ask for forgiveness genuinely from our hearts, 6. Wait for him to answer and 7. Finally, allow Him to do the rest. Ouch! This sounds much to take in. No, I don't think so. Just accepting to go this route would be hugely beneficial. Jesus Christ does not require your human effort to do the entire job, although humans would be used to a certain extent.

Remember, as Christians, each person has a stake in God's kingdom, and therefore no need to envy or be jealous of any man. When your brother is blessed, thank God for him and realize your time is coming. Be focused and help others realize their dreams. Jesus Christ knows and recognizes everyone, unlike the author, is limited, but God is unlimited. Please remember this. It is essential not to make things complicated for others because more problems are dished out when things like this happen. Today our world faced the worst epidemic, Covid 19, Omicron, etc that has never happened in the history of man. There is a cause for this. Until we realize certain reasons why this happened in every ramification, we can all adjust; otherwise, we continue to live our regular lives as usual. The persistence of our actions puts the world in jeopardy and confusion, just as we are seeing today. It appears no one can see what is happening. I believe this is the time to remember the weak ones in society because not everyone will turn out wealthy.

Honestly, I don't have the right to tell anyone what to do or offer advice to anyone, but I am just playing my part as a Christian. My tips for change-makers are to encourage you to educate your followers to position themselves better, look around themselves, and ask yourselves pertinent questions like, do you love what you see today? If their answers are unanimous "NO" then, there is a massive or significant assignment for change-makers, including myself. Therefore, interpret it in your language. Next is what can we all can do to change what is seen to bring more significant benefit to man.

On the contrary, if most of their answers are "YES", it means that you guys are doing just great then. We can keep doing the best we do in our little ways to change the anomaly we see today.

I wish us the very best in our journey because we are all in it together. Take encouragement from MY STORY!

From the quote Nelson Mandela "YOU HAVE MADE WHAT SEEM IMPOSSIBLE POSSIBLE"

Remember my past experiences have formed me to make a difference for others in the present and the future.

WHAT TO EXPECT

1. Prepare to make mistakes because it is inevitable.

ACTION PLAN

1. Stay committed and consistent with your goals and passion
2. Be aware of challenges that lie ahead
3. Continue to share my insight into the future
4. Become a blessing to others at the right time
5. Provide others support and help when required
6. Do my monthly financial stock check. The rich are eagle-eyed and miss nothing.
7. I would take this simple creed as my logo when making money decisions, no hesitation, no doubt, no surprises, and no fear
8. Ensure careful of expenditure that is likely to come up such as making a contingency plan.
9. Reliance on money should be less.
10. Draw out your SWOT – Strength, Weakness, Opportunities, and threats
11. Remain persistent regardless of the resistance that comes your way. Being resisted in any area of one life is not entirely bad but provides an opportunity to reach a new height and inaccessible places.

REFERENCES

Kurniawan, R., 2020. TA: Academic Administrative Information Security Management System Planning Document Based on ISO 27001:2013 In AAK Section of University Dynamics (Doctoral dissertation, UNIVERSITY DYNAMICS).

All verses in the bible were culled from

Holy Bible 2001. Authorized King James Version (KJV). Translated out of the original tongues and with the former translations diligently compared and revised. Thomas Nelson Inc.

ABOUT THE AUTHOR

Azubuike Onyekwuluje is a Nigerian, who hailed from the Anambra state in Oyi local government in the eastern part of Nigeria. The first son of six children, with caring and loving parents. Mr. and Mrs. Onyekwuluje. I have a great family who always wants the best for everyone regardless of who you are. Success is our logo. I had my primary, secondary, and tertiary education in Nigeria before I eventually travelled to the United Kingdom to study MSc in Oil and Gas Engineering. I also badged with MSc in International Marketing with distinction from Robert Gordon University Aberdeen Scotland. Being innovative in our time today is excellent considering the myriads of problems bedevilling us today. Therefore, innovative, and creative thinking becomes our horn under challenging times.

Printed in the United States
by Baker & Taylor Publisher Services